[lion:]

MICHAEL ZAND

[lion:]
the iran poems

Shearsman Books
Exeter

Published in the United Kingdom in 2010 by
Shearsman Books Ltd
58 Velwell Road
Exeter
EX4 4LD

ISBN 978-1-84861-115-3
First Edition

Copyright © Michael Zand, 2010.

The right of Michael Zand to be identified as the author of this work
has been asserted by him in accordance with the Copyrights,
Designs and Patents Act of 1988.
All rights reserved.

Acknowledgements

Special thanks to Alex Davies, Graham Fawcett, Jim Goar,
Harry Godwin, Choman Hardy, Jeff Hilson, Peter Jaeger,
Mimi Khalvati, SL Mendoza, Tommy Peeps, Peter Philpott,
Marcus Slease, Linus Slug, Steve Willey and Mary Williams
for their interest and support.

Many thanks also to my family for their encouragement and patience:
I couldn't have done it without them.

Cover design by Michael Zand, incorporating a photograph of an
Achaemenid era bowl copyright © Syagci, 2008.

for Carrie

[lion:]

the iran poems

five photographs:

the hunting party	15
our house at delaraam	25
the bridge	37
in a restaurant	55
young men as soldiers	75

(the moment of youth)

in a tehran park

a small boy
in red tracksuit
stands

straight
for the first time
fixed

ready
scans the flat
the scape

sees him
in the far blink . of a
blink

boro!

and maman says
run my darling run

don't catch it cold
but have a heart
a hopeful beat

you see . he is

gripping the pen . hard
and running

run and keeps
keeps it for us

Iran. Let me begin with the photographs.

When I was a child, I found them in a large brown envelope in my father's study. The envelope had a symbol printed on the front. It was the old national symbol of Iran, the lion.

Five faded photographs. To each, I give a story. To each, there's a connection to another way of life. A way of life that, having left Iran when I was three years old, I've never been part of.

My father rarely spoke of photographs. But that doesn't matter. They trigger something in me. Like folk memories, a strange world of rituals and myths. I want them to trigger something in you.

Five faded photographs. But it would be too easy to show them, so let me tell them instead. Let me take you to a different kind of Iran. Let me take you to the Iran of the mind.

the hunting party

"The first thing you will notice is that there are no photographs. They do not actually exist. In truth, what we call photographs are deceptions. Reproductions to infinity of events that occurred only once, some time in the past. This is what separates us from them."

(#1)

unwrap . faded sepia . coarse paper

background . dense woodland
foreground . three hunters . closely bunched
left. a man round . mid-cured . lined fur lined
right. an elder in a turban . whiskers
in the middle . skinny young javaan . outsized suit
in front . a sapling of a tree . a sapling of a tree
shoulder to shoulder . with shovels

my eyes keep moving to the tree

(tree voice)

rooted howls))
"i am older nower . barkened

outside there are these men with guns
branchless . with dogs . they bootpress and mash
our mud . the smell of moist . the breath of the
against the earth . harden . den spirit . no real
in this . the ground steams . an ear twitcheses . taken
out of nothing . not earthnothing
nothinnothinnothin

¡ here !
in sight in . a wolf
she found . (she deaded)

three men with dogs and guns have coldened . blood
barely shows against

beneath my hollow . dull ache strains
(time

wait for empty . wait for branchlessness
drag she . speak old prewords . hide the face
from godworld

turn . revolt . revoltion . return

¿ are she not this mud . this ghel
beshoor . ghel ra
tameez . z . z .

i really was a lion . then

where were you ?
i had to pay . to
what piece can I take with me

nothing . my son

nothing comes of nothing

*for a long time . i mean all the time
this is universal truth*

breaks it

*my memories ? mistakes ?
an ounce of decency
you say you let me bury it*

no . be hard

our house at delaraam

"Are you trying to understand? Then you are not quite there yet. You will need to look beyond the object: it is not the intentioned actions that should impress you. Search instead for the unexpected gesture or facial incongruity: this is where the interest lies ..."

(#2)

our villa . we called it delaraam

bougainvilleas glare . in the late . late tehran
foreground . my father . a lion in the door frame
a breech in the garden wall . a sheer not a cat
they believed they needed him . like you
in the middle . but not always gentle
he carries summer breathe . past simple
to nobody rises . bargard beh man

built of choob . along brief windows . openned

(the iran of the mind)

later . the small boy through it

in the villa now forgotten
(delaraam . which is
peaceful heart

encased in winter yaas
he ribbons round
sometimes i wish i was there . that

and lion is frozen in yakh
we could . sing . cocooned

¿ *where*
is the confer . runts of bird . bird
to crack the slats ?

played . the boy curves
in dusty . specks
shadow on . in places
and birds . they carry an old tune

                    balloon?

            this beautiful

                    in this beautiful

        to fly

wouldn't you like

(seventies orchestral lift music)

iran !
the land where dreams are made reality
modern desert miracle around you

straight on !
where the ancient and new work together
a brighter future built on the past

glitter !
of a backwater . now a dynamo
vibrant souls . timeless beauty

shine hard !
great pride in peace and hope
welcome . welcome

in full fakecoloured cinemascope

bullshit . this

    ancient his story
      see me asiyam now
                                      and

i will show you

          some . thing
           a little

                    soon

(west norwood)

father . old peopled now
blocked . in the west

buzzed warden like buzzard
and the walk . near to marrg
hazard hags . moist smelled drips

illudes to
an endless concrete
spirals of rheumatic rinds

illudes to
a top . butted at the place
where sons turn . pretend

like the

illudes to
a doored key . a naked entry
two worlds . twinned in heat

i am the old man . hoisting
proud
in the very best dark suit

where were you ?

the bridge

"At last it begins. We can see the image beyond the image. But what is the result? I'm afraid to say that these symbols that we hold so dear begin to lose their meaning. Yet somehow it all becomes more meaningful."

(#3)

a bridge . built by my father

in ghom . city of shrines . in a mire
foreground . lion on top
below . a steady stream of pilgrims delivering
a message . in roads to the north
by stone link across the swamp
a fertile mush . repels and repays

disaster is not known as necessary

(bridge)

the small boy through it

paces it
across and across

passing the horde on the cusp
(delaraam . which is
peaceful art

a cross

ends in great import . another
liking the habit to grow . i believe

sar garmi . pul beyneh pul
pol e ayandeh . yes a place

in the shade . for us i . dont leave
it . what is buried beneath
sounded . like fine . long . lair . lal . lam

it is all right . there . it is right

(place)

through history . but what else goes
it is a lovely morning
light adds shadows
a roun and a round
bridge in the sky frame
with how things were . once
almost together . on a
a policy of time
in the embers of the morning
moment the space to stretch
unbroken
tradition . but
lets actually find . and
through it
crumble soil around in a new
what it means . to forge yet . to
the sign unfurled . as my head
yet remind
as it in decades
the old world . lion

                                        as though

                                    dust grows . on
                                         to . on to
                                      our witness

                                         it falls

(there are no winners)

that is an lost place . lion as a faded flag

you'll never truly understand this . this
you know that don't you?

iran . like a hall of mirrors
appearances are every
the more you see . the more you think

stay blind to the the
close your eyes . and perhaps
if the ifs you have . have

the stomach for it

skinning
a pomegranate

peel in . my hard . bark

ruby . anaar . gems

but you cannon escape it

(an aside to . from the sufi saints)

the bridge . dead id
rotted to nothin . thin
tottering on wooden stakes

are you listening . i am
singing our song . the way i might have taught me
like the day we swamming . all inn nh nh

open . diffuse . youth
hear . weight . sad time
oldest . borne most . never

    imagine them as poets
    danced by tambourines
    but leaving

                thoughtseeds

(endgame)

i deny nothing

covered by a rag . is
everything that happens
within the frame

in the day
find that bed of marsh

after the credits . lion slumped

midnight is exhausted and dusty
an uninvited guest . guest

germing along an expanse of dull
as our own slick yarns hangover us

a poise . sundered of the sweet smell
severed from any "moving" finger

passed by and once past him . by
copes . left . stained by the rest

tired of the wilting swamp . made
what they say . made to watch the void

in a restaurant

"Of course there is always a defeat of time in these photographs. This is natural. Something that is dead and that is going to die. But they still offer one treasure: a photographic ecstasy. Remember they are untouchable, existing in a unique and impossible place."

(#4)

our family together . the glint of cutlery

a moment of engagement . my mother and him
she centred. but at the back . in her prime
distinct in face . naïve . certainty of expression
the rest . all in a long line . lion clinging
to one side . striking at their poses
slow to see . all mouths vague and faded

in iran the tables are long but thin

(funeral)

in the clink . in the shout
in the loud loud . laughs

and when the long song stops
the wind blows dust in my face

on a bitter hill

a man closed . in the drizzle . ex
pects
lion . greyer . coated

enwrapped

a priest . dark shadows
scarved women . (moans . lion
a dead woman . moved shadows . angels . lion

doret begardam

covereded . she . dark
so they digig . sheshovelin spirit . and lion
digig . fall toknees

doresh begardam . begardam

(crumpling)

yet if blinded . the eye of a needle
white screwed . the coursed bones of a skull
blistered . the heat from every bad blue eye
seasoned reign . an everywhere of old iran
de ceited . bug geared . sphinctered hard
a last swim in a drowned burst
gilded by thick . lie upon eastern lie
inflamed . trapped
white hot . ready read
boiled on . made out
powless . winged
under . feared
knee deep but
bad manned
made by
ama
le f
t

                                        and ask . in order to
perhaps
                        so fast . child . wood gaze

            at the screams

                of hungry men

            to the multudinous

        mass of hu

        manity

(bazaar)

in the end
we live . at the twelfth gate

bright days . sun beams
the small boy scuttles
desperately
his mother chases

like a possibility

b . arrows dodged
worlds s . l . o . w
seize through the screen
he crosses the line

reaches hype
light . pulse
white sheet for a door
ex . hales

(sanctuary)

a cold marble floor and
frontages of glass and tiles and
blue refracted light and

dull hums of prosperity and
direction . destination and
nowhere everywhere and

an eternity of echoes and
bound . ran . dam . don
a good clean break and

hunger . we splice

cool . safe and
barriered with glasses
of chai . with

amu joons and dayi joons

they hover . collect and
tee . m . or tea . m
weigh down s paceitself and

the light . lights changes
the sun is di . vi . d

dededed

the others see everything
but i am transfixed by the
light shadows of

now be is
can only see from the
outside

crowds melted . leaving
the scent of fired
unnatural metalshes

we are surrounded by space
but its now not with new
threats. purpose . screams of birth

caged in . same
i can only see from the outside
there is rah e zeebah

for a poet . a ghost
shrouded

an old tramp fool
in the cornerer
he glares

fixed . ready
to exchange words

(the fool story)

over hot sweet tea . he told of
of the forest . far from us
in those days . lion at the end
of the tracts . away so he can see
the olive groves and the village
one autumn day . the sun special
crimson sky . dust wet with warm
and as he prepared in surlience
there was a twist . turning of a cart
and beauty like simple gypsy
child . staring rigid scared
but with necklace of crusted jade
an eye to protect . worth only love
the fool clipped his donkey
with this parcel . to the house
at the top . praying throughout
when the maid answered . rushed
with worry beads . snapped
the dust picked up again and
swept a few seeds . like

                                                            the courtyard

                                        across

                        petals

            petals

                                            petals

    and petals

(he shows the way)

living on the margins
what else is there . people
maybe . false speed . but look
and the hill brings you no peace
pieces up . stinking of insane
roses drag . trains your blood
pulse pumps . beat stops for
how can i see two loves dest
so you see . it is not importan
live for the toys and . be their
and make poem . form the confluance
of birds and boards . so see in
spin . in spin . like my toddler tale
and turn in blind pursuit
slip . splash . off a new pond
submerged . bubbled
and free . unreel the light

look cram shine in to this
and emergent . bre . bre
eath . open to power the fool

where are blue sky in the night
after sunshine . warm enough

to be in side by side . and
by a tree . the tree . in a forest

young men as soldiers

"At last there is action and motion. We define the photograph as motionless, but this does not mean the figures do not move. Indeed, it is the principle of adventure and action that allows us to make photographs exist at all."

(#5)

cluster of first time soldiers . a genuine moment

a rite is performed . opportunity to attain
hand coloured faces . measures of understanding
clean matt finish . lion in the middle. young
all stared out . close to the gaze. clasping
within skin . a shudder . a jism . enough to prop
again holding a tree . cut open along its body

the place where myths . make us pang

(lion amongst many)

an ordinary day . slightly
but still there . people would expect
it . they are just . faintly
grinned . not sure for where
and how the old stories . but
are waited in front . an old gun
different hunt . too young to
say no . but ready . sarvaz
boro . sarvaz boro . all in the eyes
watch them as they
mimeeran . watch them as they
mimeeran

(control)

they wouldn't
they wouldn't
they wouldn't
they wouldn't
they wouldn't let him speak !

just cos he's slow
just cos he's slow
they wouldn't let him speak !
remember boys
he witnessed why you slept

to live in this . is to be
taken . with hoods on our heads

(arrest)

they found me in the hinterland
searching for some half meaningsin
the confusion and disorder of the broken
words and sounds . the only language
that i could now trust . they hurled me
in the back of van full of other dissenters
and vagrants . they drove us

to a large stone-soiled field . they were
shovelling us off more in despair
than hate . these were our people
every spade and tool spoke of
we had to do our duty . and our duty
was to bury corpses into the ground
but not no ordinary corpses . hero . martyr
us thousands upon thousands in lined
the stench was more than nauseous
it shone out lies . a black hole . from earth
they say . crouched dug . bent down dub

(confrontation)

lion . deliver us from this place
remember we dream
remember your own father
remember matt green floor (swept
beside the young . young olive
be side of the drak . de daybreak
de beat of the morning . lifetimes
remember the knife sent skyward
the wail of the spirit . the sun cut sap
circles fire . torn throwns prayed on
remember the tree and the rite of the sapling
makes live life fire . lights open
to the old persian myths . link us us
begun in daast . through the space
thrown by . side . the splin
ter of . to link us to the work of the wolf
and poet . to the poe . sis
given in love . remember . in the
link . rem . embers . the touch
bebin . the grain . the picture
to the daast . of all of us

(response . recovery)

shear
shear
aslan
assad

lion
lion
lion
lion
lion
lion

lion
lion
lion

<u>lion</u>

(journey)

the dirt road runs in skiddeded leopards
a long straight arid runcut . in tree . ties
each side parallel and opposed . installed
the runner paces . lion a blind man
old baba joon . praising dead enemies
strange churches defying nature to
meet outcome . bending closer each side
gravitating to central cut . closing
in the humid . a midday absolute . just
one pointed guide . swallows the old man
sees a great oak through pine thickness
it seems close . closer than horizon tails
to dismount and feel the fear of nature
it hurts proximity . guns so near
under two ancient pines . nothing grows
weighted still . in the shadow

of a circle . of deaded woods

gazed up alone to scan the sky
a flittered fereshteh . skittish lights
bathing lion in a wash of points
dance singing down the branches . enfixed
as in frail angularity he
lonely lips . the words don't work

the rite
lives in the place
between the images

in the thin cut
the edge between
the static scenes

a voice
to infinity

i am . man am
li on . as lan

circle . charkh
line . khat
line . khat
circle . charkh
life . omr
fire
light
fire
a cut
a crack
a tree i
splin . tered
a thin
stream
of glitter
you are . we
carried . in
love
lion

(the end of it)

by way of explanation

the lion falls . weight
hunters . link their arms
dance around him

there rifles . bounce up down
rhythmic against their crowns
circle of blue green

opaque. engrained . an eyes
the small boy puzzles skywards
as the old man speaks . straight

the stream is still . speckled in rays
glistening olive . so the wolf

embrace . at the heart of the day

the wolf returned . to the
garden . again west woods
scents her way . as place

by the olives . the tired old lion
settled in the earth . smile warmed
to plant her . a sapling of a

she standed above them . think long
soft of those . who dream
but never flinches she . or fears

*it's nothing . really . or
a lyric . little specks to keep . us us
a few . dyed papers . out*

*i live as we all live . to say
a few words . pass them along
that is all it is . this lion*

a reason to believe . in one

noth

and the small boy slows
in late late city
lights

sparkled cavalcade
motor veins fire . rhythms
circulate

memory will fadeded
forever and ever
to turn to machines

and the car sweeps for words
up the soul song artery
blood moon . soaked low

horizon out and out . crimson

 Michael Mehrdad Zand Ahanchian is a writer, poet, editor and researcher. He was born in Iran but has spent most of his life in London. He now lives near Reading and is a research student at Roehampton University, where he is working with Peter Jaeger, Jeff Hilson and Mark Knight.

His poetry has a penchant for the frayed edges of language, the places where tongues get tied with each other and where sometimes something new emerges. He has read at a number of poetry events, including Openned, La Langoustine est Morte, Crossing the Line and Diverse Deeds, and has participated in various collaborations with musicians and sound artists.

Other projects include his blogsite *proetics* and an ongoing international translation project called *lexico*, for which he won the Roehampton Poetry Performance Prize in 2008. He is currently working on a new creative and contemporary translation of *The Rubaiyat of Omar Khayyam*, called *ruby*.

www.ingramcontent.com/pod-product-compliance
Lightning Source LLC
Chambersburg PA
CBHW031200160426
43193CB00008B/453